P

KELLY MARKS

CREATING A BOND WITH YOUR HORSE

J. A. ALLEN · LONDON

ACKNOWLEDGEMENTS

Many thanks to my former students, now great friends and associates, for their help and advice, especially Nicole Golding on the literary side, Julia Scholes for her wonderful design for the Intelligent Horsemanship logo and diagrams and Dido Fisher, Diana Maclain, Jane Young and Hannah Rose for photographs. Thank you also to my niece Daisy O'Halloran for lending me a photograph of herself in action on page 4. Thanks to John Beaton who came up with the idea for these books and has guided me throughout. Enormous thanks are due to Monty Roberts whose generosity and support in putting me on the path to Intelligent Horsemanship has been immeasurable.

For information on **INTELLIGENT HORSEMANSHIP** and
Kelly Marks courses, demonstrations and merchandise worldwide
see our web site: **www.intelligenthorsemanship.co.uk** or write to
Intelligent Horsemanship, Lethones, Lambourn, Berkshire RG17 8QS.
Telephone (+44) 01488 71300 or fax (+44) 01488 73783

CONTENTS

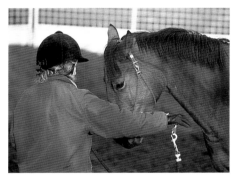

INTRODUCTION

Many readers will relate to childhood fantasies about having a pony of their own. I could picture mine exactly. We would have an incredible understanding. He would be palomino, with a long white mane and tail, which I would spend happy hours grooming. He would come when I whistled to him (a bit impractical as I couldn't whistle) and follow me around happily; forsaking all others. He would be able to jump seven feet high, but that was only when we weren't galloping around all over the place. It would be the perfect relationship. I was undoubtedly influenced by the television programme *Champion the Wonder Horse* that was showing at the time. I considered myself a deprived child because my parents didn't get me my first pony until I was eleven years old. Seamus was a little grey six year-old Connemara who cost £150. He was frightened of everything and everyone when he arrived. The only similarities between Seamus and my fantasy horse were that I did spend hours grooming his white mane and tail and we did eventually have a wonderful understanding but it took quite a time and a fair few accidents (all mine thank goodness). If I'd have had a little more knowledge maybe our bonding process could have moved along much more smoothly.

As it is not compulsory for anyone to own or work with horses nowadays, you would imagine that everyone's primary reason to be around them would be for pleasure. If you studied the situation, however, you could well conclude that altogether more complex motivations abound for many people. Just because some people are clearly unhappy in their relationship with their horse doesn't necessarily mean they have masochistic tendencies, it could just mean they went in with unrealistic expectations in the first place. Just as we may have to accept that we haven't exactly reproduced Bogart and Bacall in our personal lives, sometimes we have to admit that neither have we reproduced the equivalent of Whitaker and Milton in our equine relationship. Some people are disappointed by this, some people are blind to it. The Intelligent Horsemanship Association frequently takes calls asking for advice with horses – 'he bites me, kicks me, bucks me off, treads on me' but they almost inevitably end with the chat show style (*'My Lover Tried to Kill Me in Eighteen Different Ways'*) 'but I love him'.

Find something that your horse or pony can be very good at; for instance this pony is very good at being white!

UNDERSTANDING YOUR HORSE

In any relationship – human or equine – there are certain requirements. I personally believe an essential prerequisite is that one partner should not physically harm the other. I'd put this under the heading of 'Boundaries' and these must be quite clear to both of you. If it helps, make a list to remind yourself. Decide what is acceptable behaviour from your horse and what isn't. Remember to examine your part of the deal as well. Pain may be more obvious when coming from a whip or spur but remember that consistent discomfort from an ill-fitting saddle or the fear that a thoughtless drive in a trailer can produce can be in many ways just as bad.

It is extremely important to *be consistent* because this is the only way a horse can learn what is allowed and what isn't. Most horses are unlikely to understand why it is quite acceptable for them to rub their head on you after your regular ride but why you are greatly upset by this behaviour if you are standing him up for the judge in the show ring. I think that anyone who is in the position of making a comparison between working for a 'tough' but fair person and a moody, capricious one, would choose the former every time. There are few things more frustrating than never knowing how one can get things right. You feel a lack of control over your life and get more depressed, feeling that it doesn't matter what you do because it doesn't make any difference. Frustration can come out in a number of different ways. Quite regularly I get calls with the first line being 'My horse has suddenly taken to biting me… and for no reason at all!'

Communication

Learn to *communicate* in the horse's own language. You have to remember that horses' language is far more one of movement and gesture than one of sound. Of course, horses do use their vocal cords to communicate but it is generally to state where they are. From the separated youngsters to the mare's soft noises to her foal to the stallion's piercing scream they are mostly in general terms stating 'I'm here!' It is therefore always wise to never surprise your horse in his stable by creeping up silently but always to make your presence known with some soft words beforehand. Horses can be trained effectively to simple voice commands but remember this is our language not theirs and if we want to get on the same wave length as the horse it is essential we understand some of their language and how they view life.

Interaction

It is important to be aware of how horses interact with each other if they are in their natural herd environment. Their natural predispositions are to get along with each other. They are prey animals, meaning that in any meetings with predators they are most likely to end up as the dinner and never the diner. Survival is a top priority with horses. Keeping out of trouble and being part of the herd are very high on their agendas. Don't be misled by wildlife documentaries you see that portray horses' lives as one long round of mating and fighting. These documentaries mirror our human obsession with watching sex and violence on television. Just as the average soap opera magnifies the drama of most human lives by a hundred fold because it would be far too boring to watch what most people really do (i.e. sit around watching soap operas) so the makers of documentaries omit to show and tell us that around sixty per cent of a horse's time is spent just eating.

However, there is a clear disciplinary procedure within the herd and definite signals that horses use to communicate respect and submission. We can make use of this knowledge within our own relationship with our horses to come to a clearer understanding. The most important fact to take on board about horse communication is its simplicity. Think black and white. Yes and no. Not 'He's doing this deliberately because he knows perfectly well I haven't got time to mess around catching him today'. Horses are rarely complicated. They don't plot. They don't make long range forecasts. Their inclination is to take the course of least resistance. It is up to us to make the right thing easy and the wrong thing

difficult so that soon the horse actually wants to do what we want him to do. This is not a new concept: Catherine the Great, after the abdication of her husband, Emperor Peter III, took sole charge of Russia in 1762. No one thought she would survive but she managed wonderfully not with fear but with intelligence. 'One must govern in such a way that one's people think they themselves want to do what one commands them to do' she said. Exactly.

If you can take on board the simple idea of 'Making it comfortable for your horse when he's doing what you want him to do and uncomfortable for him when he's doing what you don't want him to do' you will be clearly ahead of the field (so to speak) in relating to your horse. I have to make it very clear here that when I say 'Make it uncomfortable' I don't mean pain. Pain is a bad tool because when fear and adrenaline go up learning comes down. Pain will teach a horse what to avoid but you don't want him to think of the rider or handler as something to be avoided. 'Making it uncomfortable' can be as seemingly mild a process as looking a horse hard in the eye and marching up to him with aggressive body movements. Or if you can work in an enclosed area (a fifty feet (fifteen metres) diameter round pen with high walls is ideal) then using aggressive body positioning and sending the horse away and putting him to work is another ideal disciplinary measure similar to that used by horses in the wild.

Using aggressive body language

JOIN UP

The process that Monty Roberts, the Californian horse trainer, calls 'join up' is central to creating a bond with your horse. By communicating with the horse in his own language, you establish trust and respect. By using your body language to influence the movements of the horse, and controlling his direction and speed, you are setting up a firm foundation for how you will later direct him – under saddle, in harness or in hand.

Join up is such a unique tool because the horse is free to make his own choices throughout. You cannot force a horse to come to you and join up, nor can you make the horse stay with you. The horse is with you because he wants to be, and that's fundamentally different from so many traditional training situations. Completing a join up with your horse means you are well on your way to creating that bond we all desire with our horse and establishing a respectful relationship from both sides.

The following is a step-by-step guide to the join up process. This is a very specific procedure whereby you take a halter-broken young horse, (see also *Leading and Loading* in this series) into an enclosed area to work using just body language. On page 14 is a section to refer to if it doesn't all go quite according to plan and information on horses that you shouldn't attempt to work with. All horses are individuals and will respond uniquely, but 'Equus' is a universal body language for horses and most equines will understand if you speak clearly and fluently enough.

Step 1 – Find a Suitable Enclosure

Join up can be performed in any safe area and the easiest place to do join up is a custom built round pen of about fifty feet (fifteen metres) in diameter. It is not essential however and, a school or manege are perfectly adequate – you can block off corners to prevent the horse getting 'stuck' in them. A large area can be made smaller by putting up jump wings and poles. It is possible to make a round pen out of electric fencing tape (switched off of course!) in a circle.

In the round pen

Use your imagination but make sure if you do use any of these less conventional enclosures that the horse would end up somewhere safe if he did jump out i.e. in another field, not onto a road.

Step 2 – Sending the Horse Away

It is central to the join up process that the horse understands that you can send him away; that he understands you can direct his movement just as the leaders of the herd would do. There are two approaches to getting the horse to move away from you. The first is done as you lead the horse into the enclosure on your long line and you unclip him, letting the horse loose and waiting until he starts to move off. When he does, you adopt aggressive body language (described opposite) effectively saying 'OK, if you want to go away go right away'. The second approach is to be more proactive in asking the horse to go away, adopting aggressive body language from the moment you unclip the long line. The first method is more suitable for the more timid horse, the second is better for the more confident 'in your face' type of horse.

Keep the horse moving away from you at a brisk trot or canter for about five to six circuits of the pen. He should be moving on respectfully, but not fearful of you. If he is moving too fast, you are probably putting on too much pressure. If he is just jogging along, he may not be taking you very seriously. When the lead mare moves other horses out of her space, she expects them to respond pretty sharply!

photos 1–5: Sending the horse away

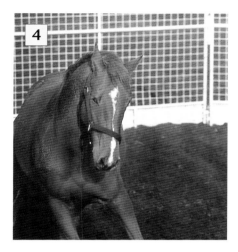

AGGRESSIVE BODY LANGUAGE

'Eyes on Eyes'
If you stare the horse directly in the eye that is closest to you it is taken as an aggressive gesture by the horse and he will want to move away.

'Shoulders Square'
Maintaining a forty-five degree angle to the horse's head, keep your shoulders square to this line (*see diagram*). This means that as the horse sees you with his peripheral vision, he will see the front of your body squarely, which is also a 'sending away' posture.

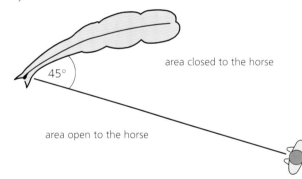

area closed to the horse

45°

area open to the horse

'Movements Sharp'
Making sharp, jerky movements, such as raising the hand towards the back of the horse, will stimulate the horse to move forwards. This can be emphasised by throwing out a length of your long line towards the horse. Always stepping slightly towards the horse, although still staying towards the centre, encourage the horse to go away more strongly. At all times be sure to stay out of the horse's 'kick zone' – the area where he could reach you with his hind legs. This would be about twelve feet (three-and-a-half metres) from his body, bearing in mind he can pivot on his forehand and turn his quarters toward you if he is that way inclined.

Step 3 – Changing the Horse's Direction

It is then important that you change the horse's direction, communicating to him that you can control his direction as well as his speed. To do this, you need to block the horse's forward movement by moving in front of him. This effectively closes off one part of the pen and opens up another. If the horse is cantering, you will need to cut straight across the pen to get in front of him. If he is trotting about a third of the pen will do. *See diagram below.* It is important that you maintain eye contact and aggressive body language throughout.

Allow the horse to explore this new direction, again for five or six circuits and then turn him back to his original 'flight path'. By now, in a fifty feet (fifteen metres) round pen, the horse will have travelled approximately a quarter of a mile (half a kilometre) which is his natural flight distance in the wild. If he were being pursued by a predator, he would now either be free – or lunch! At this stage, finding the pressure still on, and that no harm has come to him, he is likely to start giving signals (described opposite) to see if he can 'renegotiate the deal'.

Please note that using this body language and throwing the long line is an art that gets better with practise. We always encourage students to practise these things with each other before they are let loose on horses!

Step 4 – Inviting the Horse In

It is important to remember that the invitation in should be just that – an invitation, not just a sudden dropping of the pressure. You need to

Changing the horse's direction

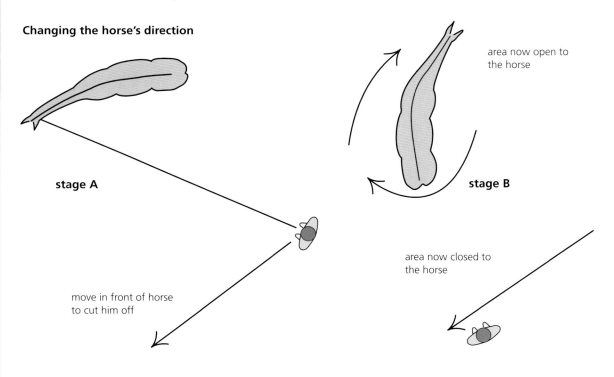

stage A

move in front of horse
to cut him off

area now open to
the horse

stage B

area now closed to
the horse

THE SIGNALS

'Ear Locked On'

When the horse turns his inside ear towards you, it will slow up his movement or stop altogether and it is a clear sign that the horse is giving you his attention. This is usually the first sign you will observe, often very soon after you send the horse away.

'Making the Circle Smaller'

This shows that the horse wants to be with you. Make sure though, that it isn't just an aversion to the pen wall that makes him want to be closer to the middle, and also that he has genuinely agreed to go away. For this reason it is always a good idea to let your horse acclimatise to the pen for a little while previously. Making the circle smaller at the start of the process may have a different meaning to making the circle smaller towards the end.

'Licking and Chewing'

He will probably lick and chew running his tongue right out. This is a throwback to what the foal does with his mother and more dominant members of the herd. It seems to be saying 'I'm just a little baby. I don't mean any harm'. Sometimes this signal is really clear, sometimes it is very subtle and sometimes you won't see it until the horse is invited in.

'Lowering the Head'

Again, this may be a dramatic gesture, with the head bobbing along the ground,or a more subtle gesture, with the horse just relaxing the head slightly. What greatly assists achieving this response is to let up the pressure in the area of the pen where the horse shows this

gesture, for he will tend to do this in the same spot where he feels most comfortable on each circuit. Finally, the horse may crane his head down low. Monty Roberts expressively interprets this as 'If we could have a meeting to renegotiate this deal I would let you be the chairman!' Experience will sharpen your senses to this communication, but when you observe the horse in this mode, he is asking you to take the pressure off, he wants to come in and 'join up' with you.

You may not see all the signals really clearly. Perhaps they were quite subtle, perhaps you just didn't see them, or perhaps the horse didn't display them. The less clear you are in your communication, the less forthcoming your horse is likely to be. It is generally not a good idea to 'sweat it out' for too long, waiting for the signals. As a rule of thumb, as long as after about six minutes, you've got the ear locked on and one other clear signal, you can invite the horse in. On no account should you continue for longer, unless under expert supervision. See also 'The Most Common Questions' on page 14.

coil up your line, and move gently to a position forty-five degrees in front of the horse's head, where he can easily see you. Adopt passive, friendly, body language: drop your eye contact completely, just keep the horse on the edge of your peripheral vision. Turn your body so the horse sees you side on, and round your shoulders slightly (*see diagram below*). Keep still and give the horse the chance to walk up to you or at least look your way and stop retreating.

If he will come to you, that's wonderful but if he stands and faces you but doesn't move forward don't worry about it. Often, horses will stand and look at you, but not take steps towards you. If this happens, you can encourage steps towards you by moving in semi-circles and arcs around the horse's head. Just a few steps at a time and then wait for a couple of seconds before continuing (*see diagram opposite*). Bring each

semi-circle a little closer to him. If the horse starts walking towards you, wait for him. If he moves voluntarily towards you and reaches out with his nose to your shoulders you have achieved join up. If he doesn't, keep circling until you get close to him, and then give him a reassuring rub between the eyes. Very often, horses just need this contact to feel confident to start following you.

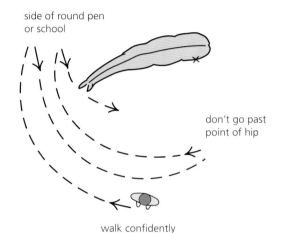

side of round pen
or school

don't go past
point of hip

walk confidently

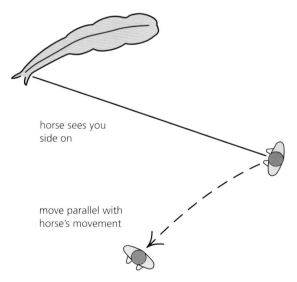

horse sees you
side on

move parallel with
horse's movement

Above and opposite, photos 1–7: Inviting the horse in and achieving join up

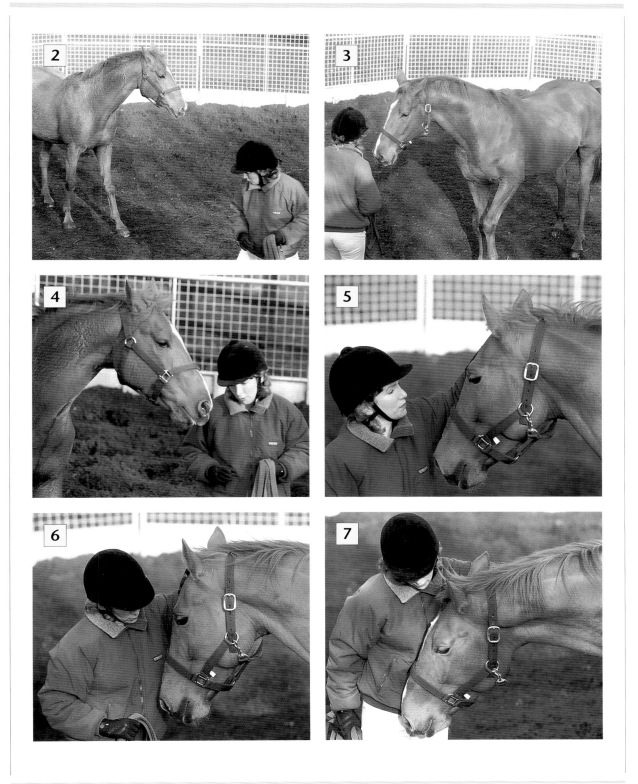

THE MOST COMMON QUESTIONS

1. 'Are there any horses you shouldn't do join up with?' First of all, as stated at the beginning of this section, I am assuming you have a quiet, well handled horse of say, two years old or more who is fully halter trained. I would not recommend anyone who is inexperienced in these methods working with any other horse except with expert help or supervision. With other types of horses you would work in alternative ways, perhaps coming back to join up at a more suitable time. The most important point to remember about join up is that it is a *tool* to benefit the horse and your relationship together. It would be totally wrong to make join up your goal rather than what is best for that horse at that time.

You certainly should not attempt join up with a horse that is in anyway aggressive. If you were inexperienced you could make matters worse. These horses are usually better off worked on a training halter until they have figured out boundaries and learned to respect your space.

If a horse was very nervous, an inexperienced person sending him away could do more harm than good. It is vital to 'read' the horse. Work to get this horse's confidence in leading and general handling first. To practise body language you could turn him out in a round pen when you feel the time is appropriate and gently go to catch him using passive body language. If he moves away, you go gently to the other side of him and turn him round so he faces the inside of the pen and then go passive again. You can continue this very gently until he allows you to touch him. When you touch him move away from him as a reward. When the time comes for join up the sending away part should be very subtle indeed.

In the same way, youngsters who haven't had much handling, could easily get confused if you weren't really well practised in the methods.

Bottle-reared foals very often don't learn their own language while growing up and can become quite 'mixed up' kids; not popular with others of their species and having no respect for human beings and their space. They need to be approached in a different way.

2. 'My horse won't go away.' You have to be very determined, and project a lot of energy with some horses. Make sure you are behind at a forty-five degree angle – getting too close to the front of the horse will effectively block him, and slow down his energy. Try throwing the line at him, slapping it against your legs or chest, raising your arms, making noises and stamping. If you are sure it isn't you being ineffective, it may be that the horse has been over-handled as a foal or perhaps you have been through the procedure too many times. Think of different ways to bring about the end result you want to achieve.

3. 'My horse keeps changing direction.' This usually happens because you get too far in front of the horse, blocking the space he was about to go into, and as far as he's concerned, you are asking him to change direction. It is very easy to overtake the horse just after a change of direction, and inadvertently send him back the other way. Remember – he's looking for a space to move into. Give him space.

Sometimes the change in direction happens because he is being distracted by something outside the pen. If it keeps happening in the same spot, make sure you anticipate the change of direction, and put a little more pressure on before he gets to that place.

4. 'My horse doesn't follow me.' Make sure that you are walking confidently, in circles of the right size. Too small a circle, and you risk cutting in too close to the horse making it hard for him to turn. Too large a circle, and the horse finds it less attractive initially to follow. Make sure you walk fluently and don't hesitate, which effectively blocks the horse. A common fault which comes from trying too hard is walking far too slowly which makes the horse lose interest. Some people lack the trust that it will actually happen and hardly walk at all. It's as if they want the horse to go first! Remember: *if you don't lead the horse can't follow*, it's just not possible. If you are still having problems try clipping the horse on to a lead rope, if he follows you without resisting the rope, then you know that it is probably your walking that is at fault. If he doesn't want to follow you even when clipped on to the rope, you would be well advised to study the *Leading and Loading* book in this series.

5. 'My horse won't turn in or make the circle smaller.' Has your horse been lunged? Cutting in, or turning to look at you, are both generally reprimanded on the lunge. Horses which have been lunged extensively, with the trainer standing in the middle of the circle, have had to learn to ignore the body language signals being given to them, and therefore often 'switch off'. Changing the horse's direction several times can help focus his attention.

6. 'How many times should I use join up?' Three or four times when starting a horse is fine, and again if you are bringing the horse back into work, or if you need to re-establish your relationship, for instance, after moving stables. A formal join up isn't something you need to do very often but remember to use the same body language every day when handling your horse – assertive when you need him to move back out of your space, passive when you go to catch him or when you want him to feel comfortable with you. A good rule of thumb is to let the horse loose in an enclosed area, and walk around. If he stays with you wherever you go, (and it's not just because you feed him titbits – a real no-no), then he's joined up quite enough.

7. 'My horse already follows me everywhere. Does that mean he's joined up?' Possibly, but not necessarily. It could be that he sees you as a fair and consistent leader, and wants to be with you as his safety zone, because the experiences you've shared have shown you to be trustworthy, and in that case, yes, he is joined up. If he's just with you because you feed him titbits, or because he likes to push you around the school, or because he is nosey, then no, you haven't achieved join up in the way that Monty Roberts who coined the phrase defines it. In any case, the properly joined up horse will move respectfully away from you when asked. Sending the horse away from you is no more unreasonable than asking the horse to trot a circle under saddle or be long-lined or lunged.

FOLLOW UP

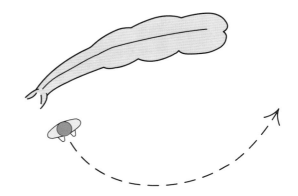

When you can approach his head give him a good rub between the eyes and then walk away moving in circles (*see diagram*). Start by circling on the right hand, make the diameter of the circle about the length of the horse, walk in a smooth, workmanlike fashion. Once the right is accomplished you can circle left. He should follow you or at least move to maintain his head in your direction. If he finds it a little difficult at first you can always give him a little 'prompt' with the headcollar, just bringing him with you for a couple of strides and then walking smoothly on. If you can achieve this 'follow up' it really means something very special. You and the horse have made a deal in his own language. You have communicated to the horse that you are his safety zone, that things are more easy and pleasant for him if he stays near you. The effects of this can be profound for both of you. I have seen horses which totally change their whole attitude after this process, in effect saying 'At last somebody who understands me'. If you would like to learn more about these techniques do see page 2 for further information.

walk around your horse in a confident workmanlike fashion

Follow Up (*Photos 1–7, beginning on page 16*).

The horse should choose to keep his head by yours as you walk him round in small circles, circling first to the right and then to the left.

POINTS TO REMEMBER

- Be **observant**. Learn to read the horse. His eyes, ears, pulse rate, tail, legs and total body language are all telling you about how he is thinking and feeling. Sometimes I have to tell an owner that their horse just doesn't understand what they expect of him. It's easy for them to suppose I have some mystical powers particularly when I can predict what the horse is going to do next. It's not mystical powers at all though. It's just observation and reading the signs the horse is giving. I can see the horse licking and chewing. I can feel his pulse rate. I can see the worried expression about his eyes. Anyone can learn to do this. You've just got to care enough.

- Be **kind**. You have the option, within reason, to make things as unpleasant for the other party as you feel like. I often see stable lads in Lambourn riding along – giving a horse a jag in the mouth here or a 'boot' there. It doesn't appear to be related to what the horse is doing at all. It's probably because they're unhappy about something else in their life and a horse can't fight back. Cowardly people will pick on them rather than the real problem. This is called 'displacement'. See 'Handling the Dark Side' on page 20. Other times you see a lad giving his horse a pat here and a reassuring rub there. Then both the horse and the human will be happier.

- Be **generous**. Keep looking for the good things to praise not just the bad things to punish. Reward the slightest try. Catch them doing something right. Seamus, my wonderful little grey pony became a star because we found something he could do really well. He won every 'Best Turned Out' competition in the area. He was good at being white. Once we'd experienced a little success at something it spilled out into everything we did together.

- Have some **sympathy**. A horse can't tell us when he's not feeling one hundred per cent, it's up to us to try and discover what's wrong. We all have off days and the special people are those who can love us even on the days when we're horrible.

- Be **honest**. We've probably all asked a horse to do something we're not sure about ourselves. In my mind comes a double incorporating the Irish Bank at Hickstead – thank goodness my wonderful old horse knew what to do because I didn't have a clue. However, if you really don't want to do something, or at least are not committed to it, and your horse picks up on this and refuses don't blame him. He probably thinks he's protecting you and it is really not fair to punish him for that.

  Be honest enough also to realise when you've made a mistake or you're just not right for each other anymore. More time is wasted and unhappiness caused by people and horses clearly unsuited. Do you like the person you are when you're with your horse? He should bring out the best in you and vice versa. If this isn't happening you are both going to be better off with different partners.

- Spend **quality time** together. Winning competitions can be fabulous. Studies have shown that people who go through a scary experience together can fall in love through a process called 'catastrophic bonding'. In the same way, I always felt an incredible bond with my horses when we'd gone through an exciting race or competition together. I can't understand people who win a race and then spend the next ten minutes shoving their arms in the air and saluting themselves when they could be hugging their horse! My competition days are over but I still get that same feeling when I achieve join up with a horse. It is lovely to spend time grooming them, taking them out for a pick of grass, leading them out for a walk, just watching them eat. Don't miss out.

- In behaviourist terms become a 'Generalised Positive Reinforcer'. Or more simply put someone to whom **pleasant associations** are made. Have you ever had one of those permanently negative people in your life so that as soon as you hear their voice

on the other end of the telephone your heart sinks? You know it's not going to be good news. Have you ever had a boss who as you drove into the car park made you feel sick at the thought of the day ahead? Are *you* that person or that boss? No, of course not – that was just a joke (honestly).

- Before going out to spend time with your horse take a few deep breaths and make every effort to put the other cares and worries of your day aside. As we've already discussed there are various methods of making it 'uncomfortable' for a horse. The saddest thing is that sometimes we are not even aware of how we are making the horse uncomfortable. What are the effects of using ill-fitting saddles and bridles so we make it a painful experience for the horse to be ridden by us? Don't forget if you've taken responsibility for this horse it means taking responsibility for every aspect of his comfort. Feet, teeth, digestion, muscles, joints, the list is endless but if he is uncomfortable in any way it's up to us to find out and get it put right. It's also essential to understand that if a person is unhappy and agitated when they go to spend some time with their horse, they are giving out an irritating energy causing a vicious circle of the horse finding it impossible to settle with them and they consequently become more frustrated.

HANDLING THE DARK SIDE

If you take a careful look round the average livery yard or show ground you will often be amazed to see a lot of angry, unhappy people. Of course, there are angry aggressive people in all walks of life but does the horse world attract them particularly – or do horses turn otherwise nice people into monsters? We name our courses 'Intelligent Horsemanship' and we feel that losing one's temper, as an uncontrolled undisciplined act, can play no part in our work and can certainly completely destroy the trust of a formerly good relationship. There have been times when I've mentioned to people that it is unacceptable to lose your temper with animals. They have more or less said that this philosophy is all right for super-humans and saints, but 'sometimes you just can't help yourself'. Whilst I agree that it may well be natural for some people to lose their temper, particularly if they've been subjected to violence and temper tantrums whilst growing up themselves, it is possible to break the pattern if you commit yourself to the decision that this is what you are going to do.

A great deal of anger comes from frustration and frustration comes from thinking that you can't handle the problem presented. But supposing you were confident you could solve whatever challenge you came across? Then you wouldn't get frustrated and you wouldn't get angry – simple! You would be able to solve any problem that you have. Look at it this way – a quiet, intelligent person thinking through and looking at a problem from all angles (this is you by the way), is far more likely to come up with a

solution than some angry, spitting, screaming idiot (not you but someone you know?).

Next time a challenge arises don't choose anger, or the easy option to just 'bash' the horse in some way. Pause and say to yourself, 'I know I can work this out'. If you can stand apart from the situation for a while, all the better. Maybe even jot down some notes or discuss possible solutions with an intelligent friend.

Be clear in your mind what it is you want to achieve. Then think 'how can I make it easy and comfortable to do what I want him to do and difficult and uncomfortable to do what I don't want him to do?'. What could you achieve on the right path in the short term?

From observation, it seems that some people feel they *should* be angry when there's a problem. Again this is a dilemma that needs analysing. Certainly if you are a competition rider you should care whether you give a bad or below par performance, but anger will immobilise you, preventing you from finding better answers. So don't chose it!

Is anger ever useful? Possibly if you get annoyed with yourself and don't try to put the blame on others it can have a purpose. I have also sometimes found it helpful to 'act' somewhat aggressively in circumstances where I need additional strength, for instance if I am schooling a particularly tough horse on the ground. Not being particularly strong or heavy, I need to put a fair amount of effort into my movements to be effective. To actually be angry though would be ridiculous.

Be wary too of 'displacement'. This refers to a shift of emotion away from the person or object, towards what one feels is a more neutral or less dangerous person or object. For example, you're upset by the person you work for so you come home and take it out on a member of your family.

Not infrequently, the smallest incident may serve as the trigger which releases all the pent-up emotion in a torrent of displaced anger and abuse. Anyone in a 'weaker' position i.e. animals, children or people who are financially tied to the aggressor in some way, are ideal candidates because they can't fight back. I bet there aren't many people who would pick on a prize boxer, saying 'I just lost my temper – I couldn't help myself', because they'd be well aware of the possibilities of unpleasant reprisals. Much more sensible it seems to 'lose it' with your horse or child – it's time those people faced up to the fact that they're bullies as well as cowards.

In a similar way, some people who are frightened of horses, or get embarrassed easily, express anger at the horse instead of admitting the real reason to themselves or to anyone else. Consequently, it is the horses which suffer until these people face up to their real feelings and take more appropriate steps.

If you find you are generally very good natured but find yourself getting irritated with one particular horse on a consistent basis, you may have to face up to the fact that you are not compatible. It happens. Do both of you a favour and find a horse more suited to your tempera-ment and abilities.

Stress Relief

Another cause of anger is stress spilling over from other areas of your life. Are you finding yourself getting angry about many things just lately? A health check should be your first stop, your doctor can talk to you about whether you are eating correctly and sleeping enough. If you are in a stressful, high powered job, you must put all that behind you before spending time with your horse. There are so many good alternative remedies out there for horses now; homoeopathy, aromatherapy, massages, acupuncture. It may be that your horse doesn't need these treatments as much as you do though!

Another important stress reliever is to work on your breathing. Correct breathing is so important on a number of different levels. If your breathing is calm, even and steady, then to a degree, the mind experiences these same quali-ties. If the lower abdominal muscles are relaxed during inhalation there is more room for the diaphragm to move down, and more air is taken into the lungs. Make your breathing long, slow, calm and deep. When you inhale, expand not only your chest but your upper and lower abdomen. You can breathe more fully and are therefore more energised. There is a strong connection between your breath, your mind and emotions. For example, when a person gets angry they tend to hold their breath and when someone gets anxious or panics their breath tends to get shorter and shallower.

Breathing is the way you fully oxygenate your body and thus stimulate the electrical process of each and every cell – including your brain cells. Lower abdominal breathing helps keep the centre of gravity low and is associated with calmness and relaxation. One of the best ways to start relaxation training is sitting or lying down meditation. Yoga and martial arts training also include excellent relaxation techniques.

TWELVE TIPS FOR STAYING CALM

1. Analyse why you get angry. Could it be frustration, displacement, fear, embarrassment, incompatibility or stress?

2. Face up to it!

3. Deal with the real issue.

4. Learn to breathe correctly.

5. Make a contract with yourself to eliminate violence as an option.

6. Think how you are going to act if there is a chance your temper could be tested. Visualise yourself acting with complete dignity.

7. Keeping your cool doesn't mean being weak. Just the opposite – you can be far more effective if you keep your wits about you.

8. Accept that people will actually admire you far more if you keep your cool. Play the admiring comments of people in your head.

9. Don't deal with the horse when you're so tired, stressed, hungry, unhappy that you know you can't do him justice. If you feel yourself getting worked up, take time out until you feel calm enough to deal with things more intelligently.

10. Don't carry a whip if you think there's a chance you are going to use it in temper rather than just as an additional signalling system. The 'wip wop' rope works better and you need to use it in a pretty controlled fashion for best effect – a good discipline for you.

11. Be kind to your horse and yourself. Appreciate both of your good points frequently.

12. Embarrassed? Don't take yourself so seriously – who do you think you are anyway!?

THE LOVE MATCH

When your horse sees you – what do you imagine he is thinking and feeling? In my all time favourite racing story *The Love Match*, the eighteen-year-old Italian brood mare Signorina had been extremely disappointing only ever having bred one foal. Her sentimental owner Chevalier Ginistrelli, who had come to England from Italy noticed that she was extremely taken by a neighbour's stallion, Chaleureux, who used to call to her as he was led past her field for his daily walk and she always called back to him earnestly. Chaleureux was not a highly regarded stallion but a handicapper with a stud fee of just nine guineas. Ginistrelli decided to send her to Chaleureux based as he put it on 'the boundless laws of sympathy and love'. The result of this 'love match' was a little filly which Ginistrelli named 'Signorinetta'. With no successful horses in his stables and being a foreigner to boot Ginistrelli was a laughing stock in English racing circles.

When Signorinetta cantered in to win the 1908 Epsom Derby priced at 100 to 1 it was at first greeted with a stunned silence but when the Chevalier, wearing an ancient panama hat danced out on to the course , both he and the filly were afforded a reception they thoroughly deserved. Two days later Signorinetta

won the Oaks. The King sent for the Chevalier after the race and led him to the front of the Royal Box where they were both received with tumultuous cheering. I just loved the description her tearful owner gave of how he felt about his little filly: 'She's the Child of my Heart – she's everything that's good'. Is that how your horse thinks of you?

'Winning can be great.' Kelly on Crackling after winning the Trinifold Silver Crest at Newbury. The whip was carried but certainly not used.

Photo Credits

The author wishes to express her sincere thanks to David Miller,
Diana Maclain, Francis Tillemans, Hannah Rose, *Horse and Rider,*
Paddock Studios, Dido Fisher, Jane Young and John Britter for
supplying photographs for this book.

British Library Cataloguing-in-Publication Data.
A catalogue record for this book is available from the British Library

ISBN 0.85131.795.2

© Kelly Marks 2000

Published in Great Britain in 2000 by
J. A. Allen an imprint of Robert Hale Ltd.,
Clerkenwell House, 45–47 Clerkenwell Green,
London EC1R 0HT

Design and Typesetting by Paul Saunders
Series editor John Beaton
Diagrams by Julia Scholes and Rodney Paull
Colour processing by Tenon & Polert Colour Scanning Ltd., Hong Kong
Printed in Hong Kong by Dah Hua Printing Press Co. Ltd.